TIMELINE *of the* COLONIAL WORLD

By Charlie Samuels

Gareth Stevens
Publishing

Please visit our Web site www.garethstevens.com. For a free color catalog of all our high-quality books, call toll free 1-800-542-2595 or fax 1-877-542-2596.

Library of Congress Cataloging-in-Publication Data
Samuels, Charlie, 1961-
 A timeline of the colonial world / Charlie Samuels.
  p. cm. — (History highlights)
 Includes index.
 ISBN 978-1-4339-3495-7 (library binding)
 ISBN 978-1-4339-3496-4 (pbk.)
 ISBN 978-1-4339-3497-1 (6-pack.)
 1. Colonies—America. 2. Colonies—Australia. 3. Colonies—Africa. 4. Europe—Territorial expansion. I. Title.
JV221.S26 2010
 909'.0971200202—dc22   2009042093

Published in 2010 by
Gareth Stevens Publishing
111 East 14th Street, Suite 349
New York, NY 10003

© 2010 The Brown Reference Group Ltd.

For Gareth Stevens Publishing:
Art Direction: Haley Harasymiw
Editorial Direction: Kerri O'Donnell

For The Brown Reference Group Ltd:
Editorial Director: Lindsey Lowe
Managing Editor: Tim Cooke
Editor: Ben Hollingum
Children's Publisher: Anne O'Daly
Design Manager: David Poole
Designer: Karen Perry
Picture Manager: Sophie Mortimer
Production Director: Alastair Gourlay

Picture Credits:
Front Cover: Topfoto: The Granger Collection:

istockphoto: 13, 15t, 16, 18, 27b, 29; Compass and Camera: 22; Falataya: 21; Mike Rega: 27t; Tommy Images: 23; Jupiter Images: Ablestock: 34, 42; Photos.com: 10, 11, 19, 20, 31, 35t, 37, 39b, 41, 43, 45; Stockxpert: 5, 6, 7, 9, 12, 14, 24, 25, 33t, 35b, 38; Topfoto: 30; The Granger Collection: 26

All Artworks Brown Reference Group

Publisher's note to educators and parents: Our editors have carefully reviewed the Web sites that appear on p. 47 to ensure that they are suitable for students. Many Web sites change frequently, however, and we cannot guarantee that a site's future contents will continue to meet our high standards of quality and educational value. Be advised that students should be closely supervised whenever they access the Internet.

Manufactured in the United States of America
1 2 3 4 5 6 7 8 9 12 11 10

CPSIA compliance information: Batch #BRW0102GS: For further information contact Gareth Stevens, New York, New York at 1-800-542-2595.

Contents

Introduction

For two centuries, European nations set up colonies around the world. Many achieved independence. Others remained under foreign rule into the twentieth century.

The arrival of Christopher Columbus in the Americas in 1492 marked a new kind of conquest. The Spaniards set up colonies in which Europeans governed a region and its peoples on behalf of Spain. The Spanish colonies in South and Central America grew wealthy—they were soon followed by colonies in North America, where the British and French became dominant. In the late eighteenth century, colonial Americans turned against their British rulers and won independence. Only a generation later, the young United States encouraged rebellions that freed Latin America from centuries of Spanish rule.

Asia and Africa

Meanwhile, Europeans ventured east in search of goods such as spices. Columbus was actually trying to find a route to the Spice Islands of Indonesia when he reached the Americas. The Dutch and Portuguese took the lead in setting up colonies in Southeast Asia, while the French and British competed for control in India. The British eventually established rule over much of the subcontinent; later they did the same in Australia. The late nineteenth century saw the European nations join an undignified "scramble" to assert their influence in the last continent untouched by colonialism—Africa.

About This Book

This book focuses on colonization from about 1500 to 1900. It contains two different types of timelines. Along the bottom of the pages is a timeline that covers the whole period. It lists key events and developments, color-coded by region. Each chapter also has its own timeline, running vertically down the sides of the pages. This timeline provides more specific details about the particular subject of the chapter.

Missions like this one in California were a common feature of Spanish colonialism in the Americas. They often combined the roles of church and fortress. ↓

In the Wake of Columbus

After Columbus, many more intrepid seafarers set
sail from Europe in search of new ports for trade and
new lands to control.

The desire to find
routes to sources of
spices inspired much
exploration. →

TIMELINE
1500–1520

1500 Portuguese explorer Pedro Álvarez Cabral claims Brazil for Portugal.

1501 The Spanish introduce the plantation system of farming to the New World, growing sugarcane in Hispaniola.

1509 A naval victory wins the Portuguese control of the Indian Ocean and the spice trade.

1500

1505

KEY:

Americas

Asia

Africa and Oceania

c.1500 Peru's Inca Empire reaches its peak under Huayna Capac.

1502 Montezuma II becomes the last Aztec emperor of Mexico.

1505 The first African slaves arrive in the Americas, at Santo Domingo, starting the transatlantic slave trade.

1508 The Spanish conquer Puerto Rico.

Portugal led exploration in the sixteenth century. In 1511, Afonso de Albuquerque seized Malacca in Malaysia, a key center of the East Indian spice trade. Sailing from Goa on India's west coast, the Portuguese discovered the "Spice Islands" (the Moluccas, now part of Indonesia). By 1557, Portugal had founded a base at Macao, on China's south coast. Japan's isolation ended when Portuguese merchants landed there in 1542. The supremacy of Portugal's trading empire was not challenged until the rise of the Dutch and British East India Companies in the following century.

Crossing the Globe

In 1519, the Portuguese explorer Ferdinand Magellan sailed in the service of Spain. He traveled to the tip of South America and through the strait now named for him. Crossing the Pacific, he pioneered a new westward route from Europe to the East Indies. Although Magellan himself was killed in the Philippines, one of his ships went on to complete the first circumnavigation of the world in 1522.

AMERIGO VESPUCCI

Timeline of Exploration

1500 Portuguese explorers led by Pedro Álvarez Cabral discover Brazil.

1507 A German cartographer names America in honor of Amerigo Vespucci.

1509 Francisco de Almeida gains control of the Indian Ocean for Portugal.

1513 An expedition led by Vasco Nuñez de Balboa claims the Pacific Ocean for Spain.

1519 Ferdinand Magellan sails through the Magellan Strait and discovers the western route to the East Indies.

1522 China expels the Portuguese for piracy.

← Amerigo Vespucci's name was given to America by German mapmaker Martin Waldseemüller.

1510 Goa on the west coast of India becomes a Portuguese colony.

1513 The conquistador Juan Ponce de León claims Florida for Spain.

1517 Portuguese sailors discover the island of Taiwan off the coast of China.

1519 Portuguese sailor Ferdinand Magellan leaves Spain to find a route to the Spice Islands; one of his ships eventually sails around the world.

1515

1520

1513 Spaniards led by Vasco Nuñez de Balboa cross the Isthmus of Darien in Panama and see the Pacific Ocean.

1518 Spanish authorities grant a licence permitting 4,000 African slaves to be imported into the New World.

1519 Conquistador Hernán Cortés sets out from Cuba to conquer the Aztec Empire in Mexico.

Timeline (continued)

1531 An international stock exchange makes Antwerp the center of European trade.

1557 Portugal establishes a settlement at Macau in China.

1570 Nagasaki in Japan is opened up to foreign trade.

1576 Antwerp's importance wanes in favor of Amsterdam.

1595 An expedition to the East Indies marks the start of the Dutch trading empire.

1600 The English East India Company is founded in India.

➔ In 1522, a ship from the fleet of Ferdinand Magellan completed the first circumnavigation of the world.

Exploring the Americas

Like Columbus, Amerigo Vespucci was an Italian working for Spain. On his second trip to America, from 1499 to 1500, he sighted the mouth of the Amazon River. On later voyages, this time on Portugal's behalf, he explored the coast of what is now Brazil.

Vespucci was one of the first people to promote the idea that the New World was not part of the Indies, as Columbus believed, but a seperate continent. Mapmakers duly named it "America" in his honor.

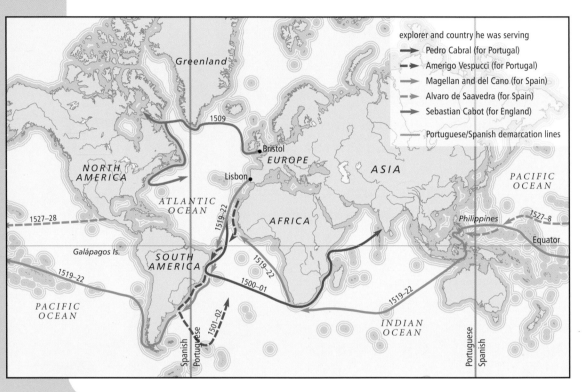

TIMELINE 1520–1540

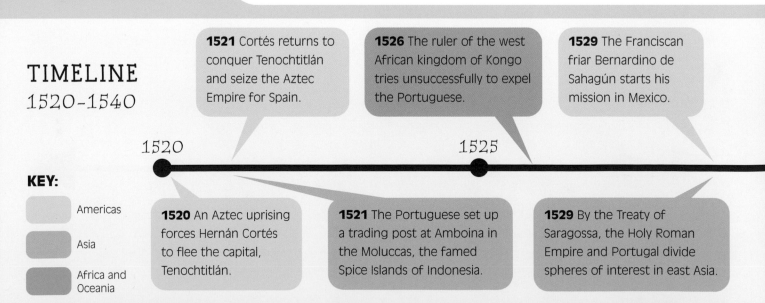

1521 Cortés returns to conquer Tenochtitlán and seize the Aztec Empire for Spain.

1526 The ruler of the west African kingdom of Kongo tries unsuccessfully to expel the Portuguese.

1529 The Franciscan friar Bernardino de Sahagún starts his mission in Mexico.

1520

1525

KEY:

Americas

Asia

Africa and Oceania

1520 An Aztec uprising forces Hernán Cortés to flee the capital, Tenochtitlán.

1521 The Portuguese set up a trading post at Amboina in the Moluccas, the famed Spice Islands of Indonesia.

1529 By the Treaty of Saragossa, the Holy Roman Empire and Portugal divide spheres of interest in east Asia.

The Portuguese built this wharf for their colony in Macao in southern China.

The Spanish were eager to exploit the New World's riches. Alonso de Ojeda, who had sailed with Columbus and Vespucci, claimed northeastern South America for Spain in 1509. Two years later, Vasco Nuñez de Balboa founded Darien (present-day Panama). Balboa crossed the Central American isthmus. On September 29, 1513, he became the first European to see the Pacific Ocean. That disproved Columbus's claim to have reached India.

So far, Spain's American settlements were on a small scale. Soon, however, more ambitious explorers were to seize Mexico and Peru, ushering in the age of the conquistadors.

A Taste for Spices

Spices were prized in Europe as flavorings for food. In Europe, the trade was run by Venice. The desire for direct access to spices drove exploration in the sixteenth century. The Portuguese began to ship pepper from India, cinnamon from Sri Lanka, nutmeg and cloves from the Moluccas, and ginger from China. To cut costs, they based their trade in Antwerp and Amsterdam. By 1530, Antwerp was Europe's richest city.

Cinnamon was one of the most valuable spices for Europeans.

1532 Spanish conquistador Francisco Pizarro conquers Peru and imprisons the last Inca emperor before executing him.

1534 The first African slaves arrive in Brazil.

1534 Frenchman Jacques Cartier becomes the first European to reach the St. Lawrence River in Canada.

1535

1538 The Spanish establish an archbishopric in Colombia, the first in the New World.

1538 The Ottoman navy and a local army combine to drive the Portuguese from one of their colonies in India.

1540

The Conquistadors

Following the European discovery of the New World, sizable numbers of Spanish soldiers and adventurers crossed the Atlantic Ocean in search of gold and glory.

Natives build Mexico City on top of the ruined Aztec capital. →

TIMELINE
1540–1560

1542 By the Laws of the Indies, the Spanish abolish *encomienda*, the right of colonists to force natives to labor for them.

1545 The richest silver mine in the Americas opens at Potosí in what is now Bolivia.

1548 The Ottomans win back the port of Aden from the Portuguese.

1540

1545

KEY:

Americas

Asia

Africa and Oceania

1540 Francisco Vázquez de Coronado begins an expedition into what is now the American Southwest.

1542 Portuguese sailors involved in a shipwreck accidentally become the first Europeans to land in Japan.

1549 Jesuit missionaries led by St. Francis Xavier reach Japan.

Many of the adventurers went only to their deaths, but other conquistadors—from the Spanish word for "conquerors"—changed the course of history. One group under Hernán Cortés conquered the Aztec Empire of Mexico, while another under Francisco Pizarro became masters of the Inca Empire of Peru. The Hispanic Empire they created lasted for 400 years and made Spain itself for a century the wealthiest country in Europe.

Conquering the Aztec

Cortés and Pizarro were both sons of minor Spanish noblemen who had come to the New World to seek their fortunes. Cortés landed in Mexico in 1519 with a force of just 508 soldiers. Crucially, he also had seven small cannons and 16 horses; both were then unknown on the American continent. His men had little idea of what they would find on the mainland and were startled

↑ The Spaniards meet Montezuma. The Aztec thought they might be gods.

Timeline of the Conquistadors

1492 Christopher Columbus discovers the "New World."

1494 The Treaty of Tordesillas divides the New World between Spain and Portugal.

1500 Navigator Pedro Alvares Cabral claims Brazil for Portugal.

1511 A Spanish force under Diego de Velazquez occupies Cuba.

1519 Hernán Cortés lands in Mexico and marches on the Aztec capital, Tenochtitlán.

1520 The citizens of Tenochtitlán revolt, temporarily driving out the Spanish.

1521 Cortés captures Tenochtitlán, winning the Aztec Empire for Spain.

1552 Bartolomé de las Casas publishes *A Brief Account of the Destruction of the Indies*, which is very critical of Spanish colonialism.

1557 The Ottoman navy recaptures ports in the Red Sea previously taken by Portugal.

1555

1560

1551 The first universities in the Americas are founded in Mexico City and Lima, Peru.

1557 The Portuguese begin a trading settlement on the coast of mainland China at Macao.

1559 Spaniards make an unsuccessful attempt to colonize the Carolinas in North America.

1525 Civil war breaks out between rivals for the Inca throne.

1532 Inca ruler Atahualpa is taken captive by conquistadors under Francisco Pizarro.

1533 Atahualpa is executed; the conquistadors take over the Inca Empire.

1535 Pizarro founds Lima on the Peruvian coast.

1535 The Holy Roman Emperor Charles V sends a viceroy to rule Mexico, now called New Spain, in his name.

1542 A Spanish viceroy arrives in Lima to take control of Peru, bringing the era of the conquistadors to an end.

» The Aztec Empire that Cortés conquered occupied much of modern Mexico. Pizarro sailed south from Panama to northern Peru.

« A monument to Pizarro stands in a town square in Spain.

to discover a well-organized empire with a capital city, Tenochtitlán, that was bigger than Madrid or London at the time. The Aztecs had built their empire by force, however, and the newcomers found allies among local peoples. The Spaniards also benefited from the response of the Aztec ruler Montezuma II. He initially welcomed them, because he thought they might be messengers sent by the gods, as foretold in certain Aztec myths.

Pizarro and Peru

Pizarro was lucky to arrive in the Inca lands when they had just been riven by civil war. When the victor,

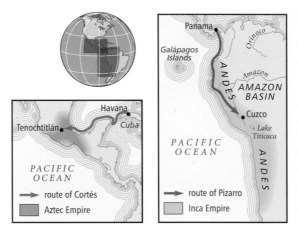

TIMELINE
1560–1580

1565 A Spanish force destroys a French settlement in Florida and replaces it with the nearby colony of St. Augustine.

1565 The Portuguese in Brazil found what will become Rio de Janeiro.

1560   1565

KEY:

Americas

Asia

Africa and Oceania

1565 The first Spanish colonists arrive in the Philippines, named in honor of King Philip II.

Atahualpa, agreed to meet him and his men, Pizarro's troops took him prisoner. With the emperor in their hands, the tiny force of 180 Spaniards was able to impose their will on the leaderless millions who had been his subjects.

Changing History

The conquistadors won a wealthy American empire for Spain; rarely have so few people left such a large mark on history.

For native peoples, though, the Spaniards' triumphs were a complete disaster. Thousands died in fighting. Millions more succumbed to diseases such as smallpox that the Spaniards carried and to which they had no immunity. It has been estimated that the population of Mexico fell from 25 million to 2.7 million after the conquest, while that of Peru plummeted from 9 million to 1.3 million.

Mount Potosí (background) yielded over 18,000 tons of silver.

A Silver Mountain

More than anything, the conquistadors sought gold and silver. Cortés sent Aztec gold- and silverwork back to Spain that became the wonder of Europe. In Peru, the Inca filled a room with gold in an attempt to ransom their emperor from Pizarro. The Spaniards then found silver in Mount Potosí, a hill in Bolivia. Annual silver fleets carried the treasure back to Spain. Spain was the wealthiest country in Europe for over a century until the mines ran out.

1569 The Spanish introduce the Inquisition to America, with courts in Mexico City and Lima, Peru.

c.1575 Bernardino de Sahagún compiles a history of the Aztecs.

1575 Spaniards from the Philippines visit Canton in China in the hope of gaining trading privileges.

1575

1580

c.1570 Scribes write down the Popul Vuh, a major collection of Mayan myths.

1576 English sailor Martin Frobisher explores the Labrador coast of Canada.

1578 English buccaneer Francis Drake raids Spanish gold ships off the Pacific coast of South and Central America.

Settling North America

Early Europeans in North America searched for riches or a route to Asia. By the late 1630s, however, European nations had a foothold along the eastern seaboard.

Plymouth Colony, home of the Pilgrims, has been re-created in Massachusetts. »

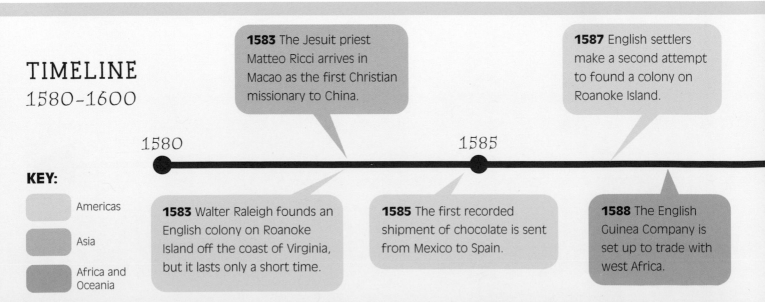

TIMELINE
1580–1600

1583 The Jesuit priest Matteo Ricci arrives in Macao as the first Christian missionary to China.

1587 English settlers make a second attempt to found a colony on Roanoke Island.

1580

1585

KEY:

Americas

Asia

Africa and Oceania

1583 Walter Raleigh founds an English colony on Roanoke Island off the coast of Virginia, but it lasts only a short time.

1585 The first recorded shipment of chocolate is sent from Mexico to Spain.

1588 The English Guinea Company is set up to trade with west Africa.

The fate of the first English colony in North America is a mystery. A settlement was established at Roanoke Island off the Virginia coast in 1584 and was reinforced in 1587. Yet when a relief party arrived three years later, no trace survived of the 120 inhabitants.

Early Struggles

Violence, illness, or famine were all threats to early colonists. English settlers at Jamestown, founded in Virginia in 1607, faced malaria, hostile Native Americans, and hunger. They almost gave up. The planting of tobacco eventually assured the colony's prosperity. By 1619, some 50,000 pounds (22,500 kg) of tobacco were being exported to England. A more sinister trade began the same year when the first African slaves were landed from a Dutch ship. But life in Jamestown remained fragile; in 1622, a massive attack by a native alliance known as the Powhatan Confederacy left 350 men,

Relations between Europeans and natives were often hostile. This weather vane shows a warrior.

Timeline of Settling North America

1566 The Spanish found St. Augustine, the first permanent European settlement on mainland North America.

1584 The English found a colony on Roanoke Island, Virginia; all trace of it has disappeared by 1590.

1607 The first permanent English settlement is founded at Jamestown, Virginia.

1608 French explorer Samuel de Champlain founds New France at Quebec.

1619 The first elections are held in the colonies when 22 burgesses are elected to the Virginia Assembly by popular vote in Jamestown.

This quarter marks 400 years since the founding of Jamestown, Virginia.

1594 The Portuguese are in control of most of the coast of Angola.

1595 The English buccaneer Francis Drake raids Panama, the heart of Spain's overseas trade.

1595

1600

1591 The English colony on Roanoke Island is found abandoned.

1595 The English adventurer Walter Raleigh sails up the Orinoco River.

1596 The Dutch set up a trading base on the island of Mauritius in the Indian Ocean.

Timeline (continued)

1620 The Pilgrims arrive at Cape Cod, Massachusetts, aboard the *Mayflower*.

1622 The Powhatan Confederacy attacks European settlements in Virginia.

1624 Dutch merchants establish Fort Orange (Albany) on the Hudson River to trade furs with the Iroquois Confederacy.

1626 Fort Amsterdam (New Amsterdam) is founded by the Dutch on Manhattan Island.

1630 A large expedition from England founds Boston, Massachusetts, and six other towns nearby.

1637 Mystic, Connecticut, is destroyed by a mixed native force, and over 600 inhabitants are massacred.

↑ Champlain and his native allies clash with Iroquois warriors in 1609.

women, and children dead. In turn, imported diseases such as smallpox, typhoid, and malaria took a terrible toll on the native population.

Around the same time, French settlers under Samuel de Champlain clashed with the Iroquois near the Great Lakes. Yet Champlain forged trading links with the Iroquois' enemies, the Huron and Algonquian peoples. The alliance would help the French in their war against the English in the next century.

The Northeast

European settlement began to focus on the Northeast from the 1620s on. In 1626, Peter Minuit, acting for the Dutch West India Company, bought Manhattan Island from the local Wappinger people and founded the town of New Amsterdam (later New York). The wider colony of New Netherland arose in the area between the

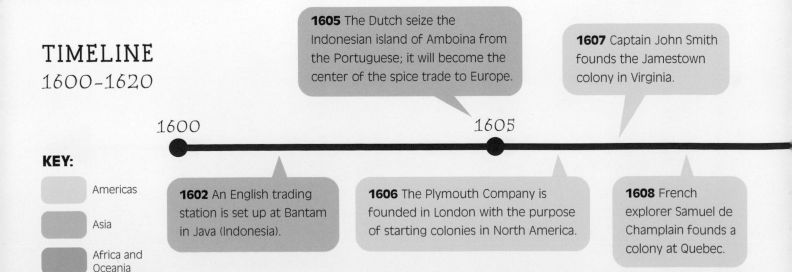

TIMELINE
1600–1620

1605 The Dutch seize the Indonesian island of Amboina from the Portuguese; it will become the center of the spice trade to Europe.

1607 Captain John Smith founds the Jamestown colony in Virginia.

1600   1605

KEY:

Americas

Asia

Africa and Oceania

1602 An English trading station is set up at Bantam in Java (Indonesia).

1606 The Plymouth Company is founded in London with the purpose of starting colonies in North America.

1608 French explorer Samuel de Champlain founds a colony at Quebec.

Hudson and Connecticut rivers but never thrived, as the Dutch neglected it in favor of their East Asian interests.

Commercial concerns drove the earliest settlements, but a different kind of settler soon arrived in growing numbers. Fleeing persecution in England, Puritan religious dissenters sailed for the New World to create a community where they could practice their faith freely. These Pilgrims founded the Plymouth Colony on Cape Cod in 1620. The Mayflower Compact, named for their ship, agreed to set up a "civil body politic" based on the will of the majority. It was an early expression of American democracy.

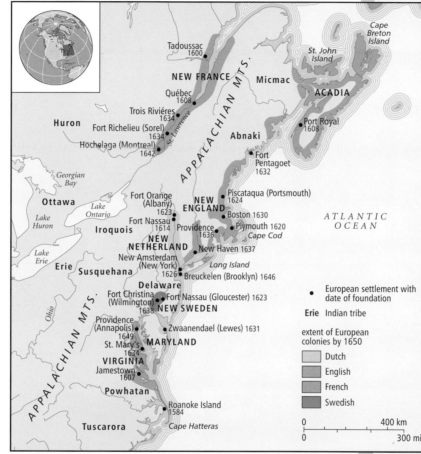

Timeline (continued)

1643 The New England Confederation is founded for defense against Dutch and French settlers and hostile native peoples.

1664 English troops seize New Amsterdam and rename it New York.

1675 Chief Metacomet, also known as King Philip, leads an uprising against New England settlements, killing some 600 colonists.

1681 William Penn begins to establish Quaker colonies in North America.

Settlers from England, France, Sweden, and the Netherlands began colonies on the East Coast.

1610 The first Dutch settlers found the colony of New Amsterdam (New York) on Manhattan Island.

1615 Rubber and drinking chocolate are first exported from the Americas to Europe.

1619 Settlers at Hampton, Virginia, celebrate the first Thanksgiving Day.

1619 Batavia (now Jakarta) on Java becomes the center for the Dutch East India Company in Southeast Asia.

1615

1620

1612 Forces of the English East India Company defeat a Portuguese fleet off Gujarat, West India, and set up the first permanent trading post ("factory") in India at Surat.

1616 The English become involved in the Southeast Asia spice trade in the Moluccas, despite clashes with Dutch traders.

1619 The first shipment of African laborers arrive in Jamestown, Virginia, beginning the slave trade in North America.

The Slave Trade

Between the fifteenth and nineteenth centuries, some 12 million mostly African men, women, and children were shipped to the Americas as slaves.

Slaves are loaded onto a ship for the "Middle Passage." →

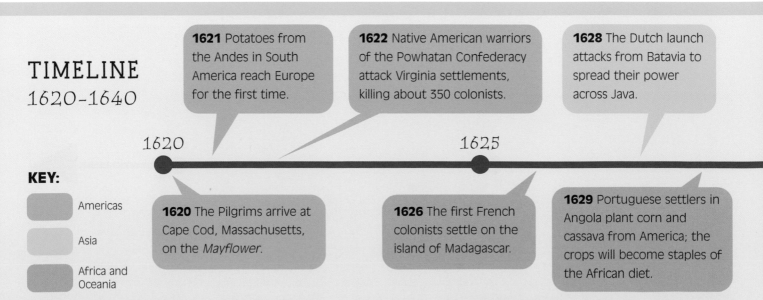

TIMELINE
1620–1640

1620 The Pilgrims arrive at Cape Cod, Massachusetts, on the *Mayflower*.

1621 Potatoes from the Andes in South America reach Europe for the first time.

1622 Native American warriors of the Powhatan Confederacy attack Virginia settlements, killing about 350 colonists.

1626 The first French colonists settle on the island of Madagascar.

1628 The Dutch launch attacks from Batavia to spread their power across Java.

1629 Portuguese settlers in Angola plant corn and cassava from America; the crops will become staples of the African diet.

1620

1625

KEY:

Americas

Asia

Africa and Oceania

↑ Slaves are sold to their new owners at an auction in the American colonies.

S lavery was an accepted feature of life in the Old World in the Middle Ages. Christian and Islamic traditions both allowed it. Conquered peoples and those who had lost their rights by criminality or debt were bought and sold. Slaves worked as labor in agriculture, in domestic service, or as artists, craftworkers, or scribes. In Islamic societies, slaves made up most of the armed forces and civil service; many became powerful.

In 1441, a Portuguese ship sailed to Africa specifically to bring back slaves. The traffic would build only slowly, and the boom years would not get underway until the seventeenth century. Then the opening of the Americas created a demand for huge amounts of labor.

Timeline of the Slave Trade

1441 The first shipment of slaves from west Africa arrives in Europe.

1619 The first Africans to reach the New World are sold as slaves in Virginia.

1662 Slaveowning becomes legal in Virginia Colony.

c.1700 Around 25,000 slaves a year are being shipped to the Americas.

1705 Virginia's Slave Code strips slaves of all rights, including the right to life.

1712 A slave revolt breaks out in New York City.

c.1780 Around 80,000 slaves are taken to the Americas every year.

1791 Toussaint L'Ouverture leads a slave uprising in the French colony of Saint-Domingue (Haiti).

1636 The Japanese force all foreigners in Japan to live on an artificial island in Nagasaki harbor.

1638 The first printing press in North America is set up in Cambridge, Massachusetts.

1639 The English East India Company founds a trading base at Fort St. George on the southeastern coast of India.

1635

1640

1632 French settlers found Acadia (modern Nova Scotia, Canada).

1636 Harvard University, the oldest university in the United States, is founded at Cambridge, Massachusetts.

1638 French settlers on the Senegal River begin to participate in the transatlantic slave trade.

Timeline (continued)

1807 The tide turns as Britain bans the slave trade; the United States does the same in 1808, but owning slaves is still allowed.

1820 The U.S. Congress passes the Missouri Compromise, an attempt to keep the balance between slave and nonslave states.

1861 After the election of an antislavery president, Abraham Lincoln, Southern states leave the Union, starting the Civil War.

1863 Lincoln's Emancipation Proclamation frees all slaves in Confederate-held territory.

At first European criminals or debtors were enslaved. But with vast and fertile areas waiting to be worked in the American South, in Cuba and other Caribbean islands, and in Brazil, the need for plantation labor quickly grew.

Three-Way Trade

By 1700, a "triangular trade" had become well established in the Atlantic. On the first leg, ships sailed from the ports of Europe, laden with manufactured goods, guns, and trinkets. The vessels were met on the African coast by local slavers. The slavers traded captives they had seized or bought from local chiefs. The second side of the triangle was the notorious "middle

⇐ African slaves pan for diamonds in a Portuguese colony in Brazil.

TIMELINE
1640–1660

1642 French settlers found Ville de Marie in Canada, later renamed Montreal.

1643 Connecticut, Massachusetts Bay, Plymouth, and New Haven colonies form a defensive alliance, the New England Confederation.

1647 The first English colony is founded in Myanmar (Burma).

1640   1645

1641 The governors of Massachusetts Bay Colony draw up a code of laws, including making slavery legal.

1642 Dutch explorer Abel Tasman becomes the first European to sight Van Dieman's Land (later Tasmania) and New Zealand.

1648 A Catholic cult begins in the Americas centered on the Virgin of Guadalupe in Mexico City.

KEY:

Americas

Asia

Africa and Oceania

passage": Slaves were shackled and packed below decks in the hundreds. One-sixth of the slaves died on the journey. Those who survived were sold to their new owners in the Americas. The third side of the triangle was the passage back to Europe, carrying cotton, sugar, tobacco, and other plantation produce bought with the proceeds of the sale.

For the merchants who financed the trips, the trade could be highly profitable. England also benefited generally from the supply of cheap raw materials and the demand for manufactured goods in Africa and the American colonies. Ports like Bristol and Liverpool sent out some 40 slave ships a year by 1750. They grew rich. But the trade caused disruption and depopulation in western Africa, while America inherited a problem that would lead the nation to tear itself apart a century later in the Civil War.

Up to 200 slaves at a time could be held in the "Slave House." ⬇

The Slave House

Off the coast of Senegal in West Africa is the island of Gorée. It was a center of the slave trade for 300 years. Traders held slaves there to await a ship. There was no chance of escape. Gorée belonged at different times to Portugal, France, and Britain. Hundreds of thousands of people were brought to Gorée in chains to await shipment overseas. Today's "Slave House" was built in 1780.

1652 Dutch settlers found a colony at Cape Town, South Africa.

1655 England takes Jamaica from Spain.

1658 Fort St. George, the future Madras, becomes the overall headquarters of East India Company operations in India.

1655

1660

1652 Omani Arabs capture Zanzibar from Portugal.

1655 Peter Stuyvesant, the Dutch governor of New Netherland, expels the Swedish colonists of New Sweden (Delaware).

1658 After a 20-year struggle, the Dutch win the coastal region of Sri Lanka from the Portuguese; the inland kingdom of Kandy remains independent.

Spanish Rule in America

Spain's dominance in Europe weakened after 1700, but its American empire continued to thrive. However, tensions were growing within colonial society.

Spanish settlers founded Mission Dolores in San Francisco in 1776. ⇒

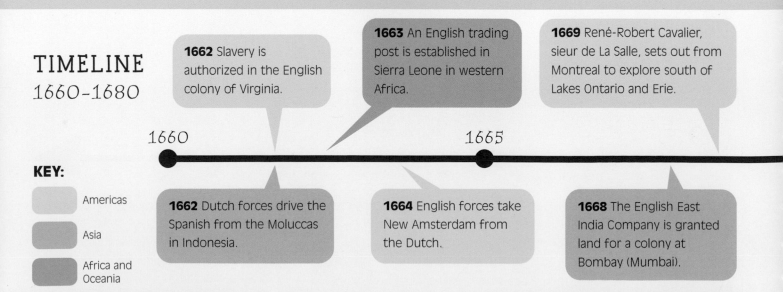

TIMELINE
1660–1680

1662 Slavery is authorized in the English colony of Virginia.

1663 An English trading post is established in Sierra Leone in western Africa.

1669 René-Robert Cavalier, sieur de La Salle, sets out from Montreal to explore south of Lakes Ontario and Erie.

1660

1665

1662 Dutch forces drive the Spanish from the Moluccas in Indonesia.

1664 English forces take New Amsterdam from the Dutch.

1668 The English East India Company is granted land for a colony at Bombay (Mumbai).

KEY:

Americas

Asia

Africa and Oceania

↑ The Spanish-style cathedral dominates a colonial square in Havana, Cuba.

E conomically, the empire prospered. Huge revenues from the silver and gold mines of Mexico and Peru were supplemented by commercial agriculture. The colonies were home to large estates owned by wealthy families. They used dispossessed Indians as laborers (peons). In 1776, the Viceroyalty of Rio de la Plata (Uruguay and Argentina) was created to exploit cattle ranching.

Early Dominance

Challenges to Spanish dominance in the Americas from other imperial powers had little effect. The empire's territory remained largely intact until the Seven Years'

Timeline of Spanish America

1702 The Peace of Utrecht gives Britain the right to trade with Spanish colonies.

1720 Texas is occupied by a Spanish force from Mexico.

1739 The War of Jenkins' Ear breaks out between Britain and Spain over trade restrictions.

1739 Conflict breaks out between the British colony of Georgia and Spanish Florida.

1739 The Viceroyalty of New Granada separates from Peru.

1750 The Treaty of Madrid sets the borders of Brazil.

1762 In the Seven Years' War, British forces capture the city of Havana, Cuba.

1763 The peace settlement following the Seven Years' War cedes Florida to Britain; French areas west of the Mississippi River are granted to Spain.

1670 England formally takes possession of the island of Jamaica.

1674 New Amsterdam is renamed New York.

1675 King Philip's War breaks out between Native Americans and colonists in New England.

1675

1680

1673 French explorers Jacques Marquette and Louis Joliet reach the headwaters of the Mississippi River.

1674 The French East India Company founds a base at Pondicherry, near Madras, India.

1679 The French discover Niagara Falls.

Timeline (continued)

1767 Jesuits are expelled from the colonies and their missions are closed.

1776 Spanish settlers establish a mission at San Francisco in California.

1779 Spain joins the Revolutionary War against the British.

1780 Spanish forces retake western Florida from British control.

1780 Tupac Amarú II, an Inca of royal blood, leads indigenous peoples in Peru in a revolt against Spanish rule.

1810 The first wars of independence break out in Colombia, Mexico, and Argentina.

Cartagena, Colombia, was attacked by the British in 1741. →

War (1756–1763), which Spain joined at a late stage to aid France. In the resulting fighting, the British occupied Havana in Cuba. The peace settlement of 1763 also forced Spain to cede Florida to Britain. Although the Spanish gained the former French territory of Louisiana in return, they did little to exploit their new possession.

Internal Tensions

Internal tensions began to weaken the empire. In the 1780s, Spain's King Charles III liberalized the restrictive system of colonial trade. The administrative system was also reorganized to increase the power of the crown. The reforms boosted trade, but they also bred resentment in the colonies.

Charles III also moved to suppress the

TIMELINE
1680–1700

1681 English Quaker William Penn founds a colony that will later be known as Pennsylvania.

1684 The English East India Company is given permission to build a trading station at Canton (now Guangzhou) in southern China.

1686 French settlers claim the island of Madagascar and build a fort there.

1680

1685

KEY:

Americas

Asia

Africa and Oceania

1681 French explorer René-Robert Cavelier, the sieur de La Salle, travels down the Mississippi River to the sea.

1684 The Dutch East India Company occupies the sultanate of Bantam in Java.

1689 War between England and France in Europe spills into North America as King Wiliam's War; settlers from the two nations fight each other.

↑ Tupac Amarú II claimed that local rulers were corrupted by Spanish rule.

church's influence. He expelled the Jesuits from all parts of his empire in 1767. Among the chief losers in the move were the native inhabitants of the Spanish lands. Jesuit missions had given them some protection from exploitation by white settlers.

Racial Divisions

The main impetus behind the urge for change came from the *creoles*, American-born whites of Spanish descent. In the racial hierarchy, they ranked above Indians, mestizos (people of mixed Indian and white descent), mulattos (mixed black and white), and others. But the creoles felt disadvantaged by crown policy. All top positions were occupied by *peninsulares*—white immigrants born in Spain. The rigid caste system was to prove the downfall of the empire after Napoleon invaded Spain in 1808. Disaffected creoles came to the forefront of movements to gain independence from Spain.

The Revolt of Tupac Amarú II

A descendant of the last Inca ruler, Tupac Amarú II was highly respected. Angry at the injustices of Spanish rule, he staged an uprising in 1780 to restore Inca rule. His cause appealed to creoles and mestizos; he also promised freedom to black slaves. After a siege of Cuzco (the capital) failed, his supporters began killing whites. Tupac Amarú was captured and hanged in 1781. His revolt was the most serious challenge to Spanish rule in the Americas, costing over 200,000 lives.

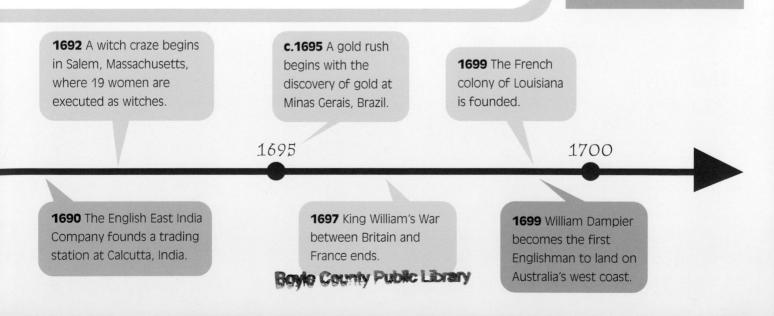

1692 A witch craze begins in Salem, Massachusetts, where 19 women are executed as witches.

c.1695 A gold rush begins with the discovery of gold at Minas Gerais, Brazil.

1699 The French colony of Louisiana is founded.

1695

1700

1690 The English East India Company founds a trading station at Calcutta, India.

1697 King William's War between Britain and France ends.

1699 William Dampier becomes the first Englishman to land on Australia's west coast.

The American Revolutionary War

In the 1770s, the 13 colonies of North America rebelled
against rule by Great Britain and created the United
States of America as an independent republic.

This famous painting
shows musicians in
Washington's army. →

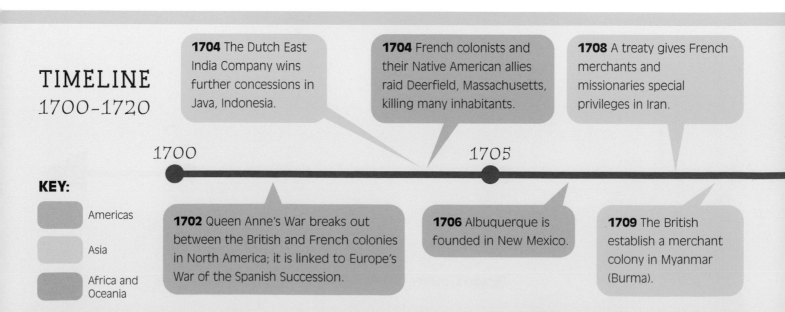

TIMELINE
1700–1720

1704 The Dutch East
India Company wins
further concessions in
Java, Indonesia.

1704 French colonists and
their Native American allies
raid Deerfield, Massachusetts,
killing many inhabitants.

1708 A treaty gives French
merchants and
missionaries special
privileges in Iran.

1700

1705

KEY:

Americas

Asia

Africa and
Oceania

1702 Queen Anne's War breaks out
between the British and French colonies
in North America; it is linked to Europe's
War of the Spanish Succession.

1706 Albuquerque is
founded in New Mexico.

1709 The British
establish a merchant
colony in Myanmar
(Burma).

↑ This stamp marks
the first clashes of
the war, at Lexington
and Concord.

By the late eighteenth century, Britain was the most powerful colonial nation in the world. But wars against the French had been expensive. Britain turned to its colonies, especially North America, to raise money.

In 1765, the British Parliament imposed the Stamp Act on the 13 colonies. It placed a tax on printed documents, including newspapers. The measure caused outrage. Many colonists refused to pay, adopting the slogan "No taxation without representation." More taxes and more protests followed. In December 1773, a band of angry colonists, dressed as Native Americans, boarded a British ship and dumped its cargo of tea in Boston Harbor rather than pay the hated tea duty.

Timeline of the Revolutionary War

1765 The Stamp Act imposes taxes on documents in the American colonies.

1773 Colonists protest a tax on tea with the Boston Tea Party.

1774 The British Coercive Acts punish Massachusetts for the Boston Tea Party.

1774 The Continental Congress meets to protest the Coercive Acts, or "Intolerable Acts."

1775 George Washington takes command of the Continental Army.

1775 The British suffer heavy losses at Bunker Hill in the first full battle of the war.

1776 Washington crosses the Delaware River on Christmas night to seize Trenton.

← A cannon marks the site of the American victory at Saratoga.

1715 Settlers push into the eastern foothills of the Appalachians.

1716 The Mughal emperor Farrukhsiyar gives special trading privileges to the British East India Company.

1715

1720

1713 Queen Anne's War ends. The French pass Newfoundland, Hudson Bay, and Acadia to the British.

1717 Colombia, Ecuador, Venezuela, and Panama establish the Viceroyalty of New Granada.

1718 Spanish colonists return to the southern Philippines, having been driven out nearly 60 years earlier.

Timeline (continued)

1777 Washington's army survives a bitter winter at Valley Forge.

1781 Yorktown falls, ending the Revolutionary War.

1783 The Treaty of Paris recognizes the independence of the United States of America.

1788 The U.S. Constitution comes into effect.

1791 The Bill of Rights is passed; it embodies the first 10 amendments to the U.S. Constitution.

⟫ The war was fought on the East Coast of the future United States.

War Breaks Out

By now, many Americans wanted to free themselves entirely from British rule. Hostility turned to war in April 1775 when rebel and British troops clashed at Lexington and Concord, Massachusetts. The first full battle of the Revolutionary War took place at Bunker Hill in June and was a defeat for the colonists. Two days earlier, George Washington had been elected to command the Continental Army. The Declaration of Independence, proclaiming the separation of the 13 colonies from Britain, followed in July.

The war at first went badly for the

TIMELINE 1720–1740

1720 Dutch settlers in South Africa move inland from the Cape of Good Hope.

1721 A regular postal service begins between New England and London.

1728 Danish navigator Vitus Bering sails through what is now called the Bering Strait, separating Siberia from Alaska.

1720   1725

1720 Spaniards from Mexico occupy what is now Texas.

1727 Coffee is planted for the first time in Brazil; it will become the country's main export.

1729 North and South Carolina become colonies of the British crown.

KEY:

- Americas
- Asia
- Africa and Oceania

United States. Washington scored a morale-boosting success at Trenton, New Jersey, in December 1776. It was not until June 1777, however, that the Continental Army achieved its first major victory. It defeated forces under General Burgoyne at Saratoga, New York.

The Tide Turns

News of this success convinced France to enter the war on the side of the United States early in 1778. Meanwhile, Washington and his army came through the severe winter of 1777 at Valley Forge, Pennsylvania. By now it was clear that the British lacked a strategy for winning the war. In 1781, their forces under Lord Cornwallis were besieged in Yorktown, Virginia. When a French fleet cut off his supplies, Cornwallis was forced to surrender, finally bringing the war to an end. The independence of the United States of America was formally recognized by the Treaty of Paris in 1783, and a new nation was born.

"We, the People"

The Constitutional Convention met in Philadelphia in 1787 to decide how the new nation should be governed. With its opening words "We, the People," the U.S. Constitution affirmed the principle of the popular will. Four years later, the Bill of Rights—the first 10 amendments to the Constitution—spelled out the rights of individual citizens against the power of the state.

← The framers wrote the world's first democratic written consitution.

1731 In Philadelphia, Benjamin Franklin sets up the first subscription library in North America.

1733 Britain introduces the Molasses Act, which heavily taxes American trade with French colonies in the Caribbean.

1739 Conflict breaks out between Georgia and the Spanish territory of Florida.

1739 French explorers head west from the Mississippi River to Santa Fe.

1735

1740

1733 The last of Britain's 13 colonies in North America is founded and named Georgia in honor of King George II.

1739 Spain's Viceroyalty of New Granada (Ecuador, Colombia, Venezuela, and Panama) separates from the Viceroyalty of Peru.

1739 Camellias arrive in Europe from east Asia; they soon become highly fashionable and costly.

The Liberation of Latin America

In the early nineteenth century, Latin America freed itself
from colonial rule. Between 1810 and 1825, almost the
entire Hispanic empire in the Americas was broken up.

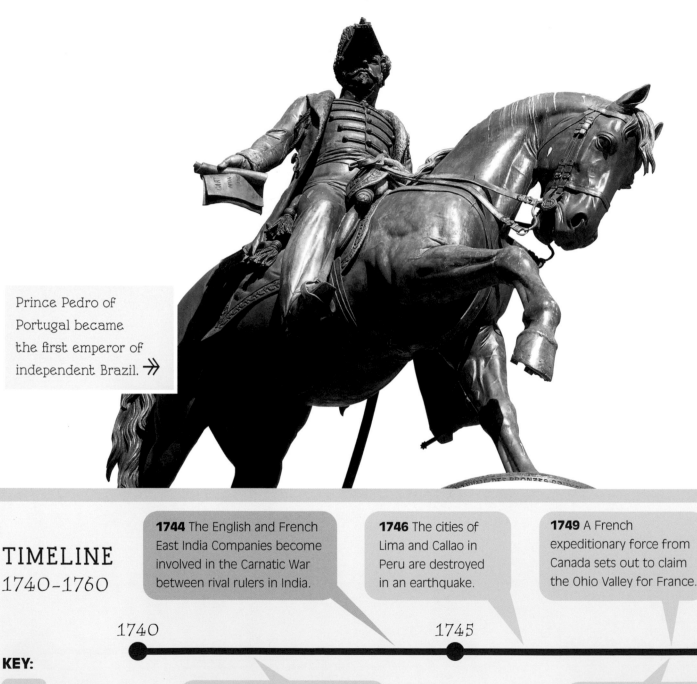

Prince Pedro of
Portugal became
the first emperor of
independent Brazil. ⇉

TIMELINE
1740–1760

1744 The English and French
East India Companies become
involved in the Carnatic War
between rival rulers in India.

1746 The cities of
Lima and Callao in
Peru are destroyed
in an earthquake.

1749 A French
expeditionary force from
Canada sets out to claim
the Ohio Valley for France.

1740

1745

1742 Coal is first mined in the
West Virginia region.

1749 The British
establish a naval base
at Halifax, Nova Scotia.

KEY:

Americas

Asia

Africa and
Oceania

By the start of the nineteenth century, the five viceroyalties of the Spanish empire in America stretched from southern California in the north to Chile in the south. Spanish colonists exported enormous quantities of gold and silver from the mines of Mexico and Peru. They also ran large farming estates known as haciendas. The native peoples were forced to work in the mines or as peons (landless laborers).

In the late 1700s, the success of the American and French revolutions inspired independence movements in Latin America. Then, in 1808 Napoleon's army occupied Spain, and Napoleon's brother Joseph Bonaparte was made king. The demands for change grew louder. Revolution broke out in Mexico in 1810, but it was quickly put down. Its leader, Miguel Hidalgo, was executed.

This statue in Mexico City celebrates Mexican independence. ⟫

Timeline of Latin American Liberation

1810 Uprisings against Spanish rule break out in Mexico, Chile, Venezuela, and Argentina.

1811 Venezuela declares its independence from Spain.

1814 Simón Bolívar is driven out of Venezuela and launches raids on the South American mainland from Jamaica and Haiti.

1816 Argentina wins independence from Spain.

1817 José de San Martín raises an army in Argentina and, together with the Chilean revolutionary Bernardo O'Higgins, leads it across the Andes Mountains to liberate Chile.

1817 Bolívar returns to Venezuela.

1754 The recall of the French governor in southern India leaves the British in control there.

1757 The British general Robert Clive defeats a far larger Indian force at the Battle of Plassey.

1755

1760

1752 Benjamin Franklin conducts experiments into the nature of electricity, including flying a kite in an electrical storm.

1755 The French and Indian War breaks out as British and French settlers vie for control in North America.

1759 General James Wolfe defeats French troops near Quebec, establishing British supremacy in Canada.

Timeline (continued)

1819 Bolívar assembles an army of 25,000 to invade Colombia, where he wins the Battle of Boyacá.

1819 Bolívar becomes president of Colombia.

1821 José de San Martín takes possession of Lima, Peru.

1821 Bolívar frees Venezuela at the Battle of Carabobo.

1821 Mexico wins its independence from Spain.

≫ By 1825, Bolívar governed an area from Venezuela to the Argentine-Bolivian border.

In 1811, Paraguay declared its independence. The inspirational leader Simón Bolívar began his fight to liberate Venezuela, his native land.

Liberation

By 1819, Bolívar had made himself president of the new Republic of Colombia. Two years later, he expelled the Spanish from Venezuela, too. Another revolutionary leader, José de San Martín, helped liberate Argentina in 1816. He then led an army across the Andes to

UNITED STATES
Gulf of Mexico
Havana
CUBA
Mexico City
BRITISH HONDURAS to Britain
MEXICO 1821
Guatemala City
JAMAICA to Britain
HAITI
1822 to Haiti
PUERTO RICO
San Juan
Lesser Antilles
Caribbean Sea
ATLANTIC OCEAN
MOSQUITO COAST to Britain
UNITED PROVINCES OF CENTRAL AMERICA 1823
Panama City
Caracas
VENEZUELA 1830
TRINIDAD to Britain
BRITISH GUIANA to Britain
DUTCH GUIANA to Holland
FRENCH GUIANA to France
Bogota
NEW GRANADA 1831
Galápagos Islands 1832 to Ecuador
Quito
ECUADOR 1822 to Gran Colombia 1830
Amazon
EMPIRE OF BRAZIL 1822
Lima
PERU 1821
La Paz
BOLIVIA 1825
PARAGUAY 1811
PACIFIC OCEAN
Asunción
Rio de Janeiro
ARGENTINE CONFEDERATION 1810–16 United Provinces of La Plata 1810
Santiago
CHILE 1818
Buenos Aires
URUGUAY 1816–28 to Brazil 1828
Montevideo
Patagonia
ATLANTIC OCEAN
Falkland Islands (Islas Malvinas) 1820 to Argentina

Spanish possessions lost 1810–25
Spanish possessions 1830
Portuguese possession lost 1822
Republic of Greater Colombia 1819–30
territory united with Mexico 1821–23
1818 date of separate statehood
— borders 1830

scale varies in this projection

TIMELINE
1760–1780

1763 By the Treaty of Paris, all French territories in Canada and in America east of the Mississippi pass to Britain.

1763 Ottawa leader Pontiac leads an unsuccessful uprising against the British.

1768 British sailor Captain James Cook sets out on his first voyage to the South Pacific.

1760

1765

KEY:

Americas

Asia

Africa and Oceania

1764 Mughal leaders are defeated in battle by the British East India Company.

1765 The Stamp Act taxes American legal documents and newspapers; protests from colonial Americans force the British to back down.

1769 Captain Cook charts the islands of New Zealand.

↑ José de San Martín still appears on Argentine banknotes.

capture the Peruvian capital of Lima. By 1824, when Bolívar and Antonio José de Sucre drove the Spanish from the rest of Peru, all of Spain's empire in the Americas had won independence except the islands of Cuba and Puerto Rico.

New Society

Liberation did not extend to everyone. Power in the new states remained in the hands of people of Spanish descent. Beneath them in society were the mestizos (of mixed European-Indian descent), and at the bottom were native Indians, who had few rights, and the descendants of African slaves. In the following decades, there were many disagreements and border wars between the new states, many of which fell under the rule of *caudillos*, dictators who held power through their control of the army.

← Simón Bolívar hoped for cooperation among the Spanish-speaking lands after independence.

Timeline (continued)

1822 Pedro, crown prince of Portugal, declares Brazil's independence from Portugal, with himself as its emperor.

1822 Bolívar and General Antonio José de Sucre liberate Ecuador.

1822 Agustin Iturbide declares himself emperor of Mexico.

1824 Bolívar and de Sucre win the Battle of Ayacucho, defeating the last royalist army in Peru and completing the liberation of South America.

1825 Bolivia—previously part of the Spanish Viceroyalty of Peru—proclaims its independence, taking its name as a tribute to Bolívar.

1770 Captain Cook explores the east coast of Australia, which he claims for Britain.

1775 The first shots of the American Revolutionary War are fired at Lexington.

1776 Representatives of the 13 colonies sign the Declaration of Independence on July 4.

1779 Captain Cook is killed by natives in Hawaii.

1775

1780

1770 British troops kill five protestors during a riot in Boston, Massachusetts.

1775 Daniel Boone marks out the Wilderness Road across the Appalachians to Kentucky.

1777 In the American Revolutionary War, the British are defeated at the Battle of Saratoga, New York.

Europeans Settle Australia

Long described as the "unknown land" (terra incognita)
on early maps, Australia was the last continent on Earth
to be discovered and colonized by Europeans.

When this 1792 map of
Australia was drawn,
the full shape of the
island continent was
still unknown. ➡

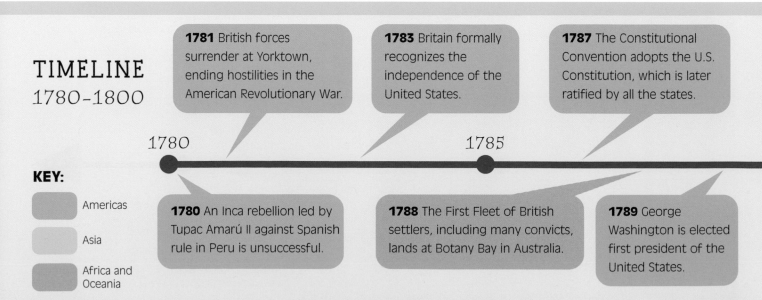

TIMELINE
1780–1800

1781 British forces surrender at Yorktown, ending hostilities in the American Revolutionary War.

1783 Britain formally recognizes the independence of the United States.

1787 The Constitutional Convention adopts the U.S. Constitution, which is later ratified by all the states.

1780

1785

1780 An Inca rebellion led by Tupac Amarú II against Spanish rule in Peru is unsuccessful.

1788 The First Fleet of British settlers, including many convicts, lands at Botany Bay in Australia.

1789 George Washington is elected first president of the United States.

KEY:

Americas

Asia

Africa and Oceania

↑ Cook was one
of history's most
skilled navigators.

Australia's north and west coasts were first explored in the seventeenth century by Dutch sailors. They called the shores they discovered New Holland. In 1770, an English navigator, Captain James Cook, discovered the continent's east coast and claimed it for Britain.

Cook, one of the greatest navigators who ever lived, explored the Pacific Ocean from Antarctica to Alaska on three expeditions between 1768 and 1779. It was on the first that he visited Australia, landing at Botany Bay near what is now Sydney. He judged that the place was suitable for settlement.

Penal Colonies

Britain's jails were overflowing at the time. Britain had sent as many as 1,000 convicts a year to penal settlements in Maryland and Virginia. But after the loss of the American colonies in

Timeline of Settling Australia

1606 Willem Jansz explores the northern coast of Australia and calls the land New Holland.

1642 Dutch sailor Abel Tasman discovers the island he names Van Diemen's Land (it will be renamed Tasmania in 1855).

1770 Captain Cook discovers the east coast of Australia; he makes landfall at Botany Bay, near modern Sydney.

1788 The First Fleet of convicts arrives in Botany Bay on January 26, commanded by Captain Arthur Phillip, the colony's first governor.

1790 The Second Fleet reaches Port Jackson; of 1,000 convicts on board, more than a third die on the voyage or shortly after arrival.

← Convicts worked on infrastructure such as roads and bridges.

1791 Inspired by the French Revolution, former slave François Toussaint L'Ouverture leads a successful slave uprising in Haiti.

1793 The invention of the cotton gin by Eli Whitney begins the mechanization of the U.S. cotton industry.

1799 The Dutch East India Company goes bust; its holdings are taken over by the Dutch government.

1795

1800

1791 The U.S. Bill of Rights is ratified as the first 10 amendments to the Constitution.

1796 The British seize control of Ceylon (Sri Lanka) from the Dutch.

1798 A French force led by Napoleon Bonaparte occupies Egypt but is defeated by the British.

Timeline (continued)

1791 The Third Fleet arrives in Australia with the first group of Irish convicts on board.

1791 A group of convicts escape from Port Jackson and set out to walk to China (which they think lies somewhere to the north); they die of starvation.

1793 The first free settlers arrive in Australia. Numbering just 11 in all, they are granted free passage, land, and tools.

1794 The first political prisoners are transported to Australia.

→ Cook entered Australian waters on two of his three great voyages of exploration.

1783, this transportation stopped. So it was decided to start a new penal colony in Australia.

Early Struggles

The First Fleet of 11 ships arrived in Botany Bay in January 1788. It carried more than 750 convicts: 568 men, 191 women, and 19 children. The new arrivals nearly starved. The land proved far less fertile than it appeared. Fresh supplies were sent for from Cape Colony in South Africa, but they were not enough. The period was remembered as "the starving time."

By the late 1790s, Australia was receiving regular transports of convicts. They were mostly kept in Port Jackson, near Botany Bay. However, some were sent to tiny Norfolk Island, a dot in the Pacific some 900 miles (1,500 km) to the east, or else to Van Diemen's Land (later Tasmania)

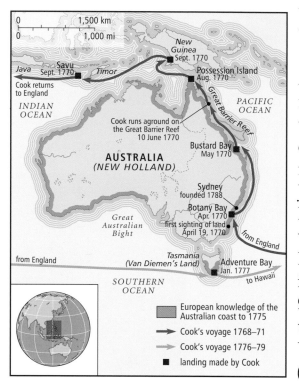

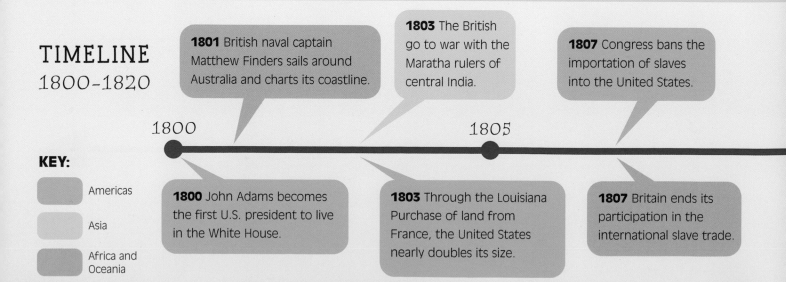

TIMELINE 1800–1820

1801 British naval captain Matthew Finders sails around Australia and charts its coastline.

1803 The British go to war with the Maratha rulers of central India.

1807 Congress bans the importation of slaves into the United States.

1800

1805

KEY:

Americas

Asia

Africa and Oceania

1800 John Adams becomes the first U.S. president to live in the White House.

1803 Through the Louisiana Purchase of land from France, the United States nearly doubles its size.

1807 Britain ends its participation in the international slave trade.

↑ European settlers
persecuted Aborigines
and seized their
traditional lands.

A Brutal Persecution

The Aborigines had inhabited Australia for at least 60,000 years. Living in isolation from the world, they were nomadic hunter-gatherers. The Europeans saw the Aborigines as little better than animals. Settlers stole their lands and hunted them down. Persecution, warfare, and disease decimated their numbers. The worst atrocities were committed in Tasmania, where the Aboriginal population was eradicated in a genocidal act of ethnic cleansing.

several hundred miles to the south.
They were put to work building roads and bridges or forced to provide unpaid labor on farms and landholdings. Treatment was harsh, with frequent floggings, and many tried to escape only to die in Australia's unforgiving outback. It was a cruel beginning for a new colony, and it left a bitter legacy of resentment long after Australia had become a place of hope and fulfillment for thousands of free immigrants from Europe in the nineteenth century.

1810 Father Miguel Hidalgo leads an unsuccessful uprising in Mexico against Spanish rule.

1812 The War of 1812 begins when the United States declares war to reduce British interference in U.S. trade.

1816 Argentina declares independence from Spain.

1819 The British found a trading base at the southern tip of Malaya; it becomes modern-day Singapore.

1815

1820

1811 Paraguay declares independence from Spain.

1814 The British take formal possession of Cape Colony, in South Africa.

1819 Simón Bolívar frees Colombia from Spanish control.

Colonialism

To secure fresh sources of raw materials and open up new markets for manufactured goods, European powers expanded their overseas colonies and created new ones.

A hotel in Victorian British style stands on the seafront in Mumbai, India. ↠

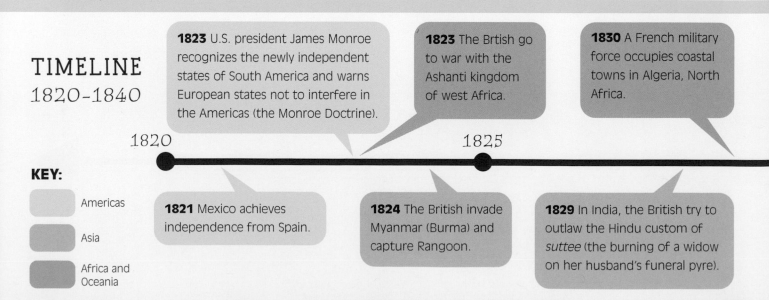

TIMELINE
1820–1840

1823 U.S. president James Monroe recognizes the newly independent states of South America and warns European states not to interfere in the Americas (the Monroe Doctrine).

1823 The Brtish go to war with the Ashanti kingdom of west Africa.

1830 A French military force occupies coastal towns in Algeria, North Africa.

1820

1825

KEY:

Americas

Asia

Africa and Oceania

1821 Mexico achieves independence from Spain.

1824 The British invade Myanmar (Burma) and capture Rangoon.

1829 In India, the British try to outlaw the Hindu custom of *suttee* (the burning of a widow on her husband's funeral pyre).

After the loss of its colonies in North America, Britain sought to strengthen its empire and expand its trade in Asia. In 1819, the colonial administrator Sir Stamford Raffles established the free port of Singapore, which stood at a key point to control regional trade. From 1824 to 1826, Britain consolidated its hold over the Malayan Peninsula. At the same time, British forces from India responded to an invasion of Bengal by attacking neighboring Burma. By the mid-1880s, the whole country had been annexed to India.

Trade boomed in cotton goods, manufactured in India or in Britain itself. They were shipped through Singapore to Southeast Asia and China.

⇑ Indian villagers report their problems to a visiting British district commissioner.

Opium Wars

A more lucrative trade in another Indian product, opium, caused the outbreak of

Timeline of Colonialism

1815 At the end of the Napoleonic Wars, a fifth of the world population is under the control of the British Empire.

1819 British administrator Sir Stamford Raffles founds the free port of Singapore on the Malaysian Peninsula, which grows into an important trading center.

1824 In the First Anglo-Burmese War, the British seize the coastal provinces of Burma, expanding their empire eastward from Bengal in India.

1830 The French under King Louis Philippe begin their colonization of Africa by occupying Algeria. The Foreign Legion is founded from international recruits to serve in Africa.

⇐ Hong Kong, shown in 1865, was a British prize in a war against China.

1834 Britain's abolition of slavery liberates about 700,000 slaves in its Caribbean colonies.

1838 British forces invade Afghanistan to prevent Russian influence in the region; the First Afghan War begins.

1839 As tensions rise over the import of opium into China, British colonial troops occupy Hong Kong.

1835

1840

1834 The British East India Company loses its monopoly on trade with China.

1835 In southern Africa, 10,000 Boers begin the Great Trek north to the Zulu territory of Natal.

1840 The British annex the Boer republic of Natal as part of Cape Colony.

Timeline (continued)

1835 Dutch settlers in South Africa make the Great Trek. After defeating the Zulus at the Battle of Blood River, they found the Republic of Natal.

1838 The First Afghan War breaks out as British forces invade Afghanistan to prevent the Russian empire from threatening India.

1852 Britain annexes southern Burma during the Second Anglo-Burmese War.

1854 France extends and consolidates its hold over Senegal, the center of a growing west African empire.

➔ The largest colonial empire was Britain's, which straddled the world from Canada to Australia.

war between Britain and China in 1840. When China confiscated the drug, Britain replied with military force. At the end of a one-sided conflict, Britain gained Hong Kong, another important east Asian base.

In Africa, British colonization of the Cape of Good Hope as Cape Colony began with the creation of a naval base in 1809. In 1835, the original Dutch settlers, protesting a British ban on slave labor, moved inland on the "Great Trek." They later founded the Boer republics of the Transvaal and Orange Free State. Tension

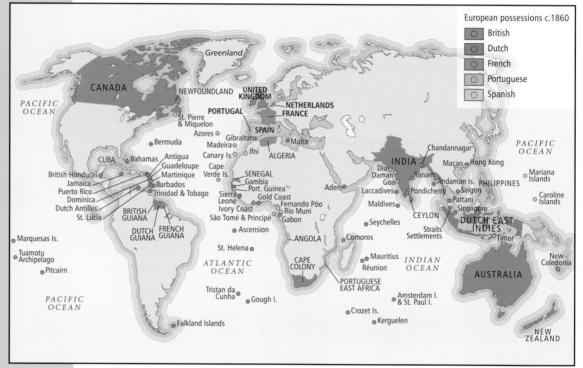

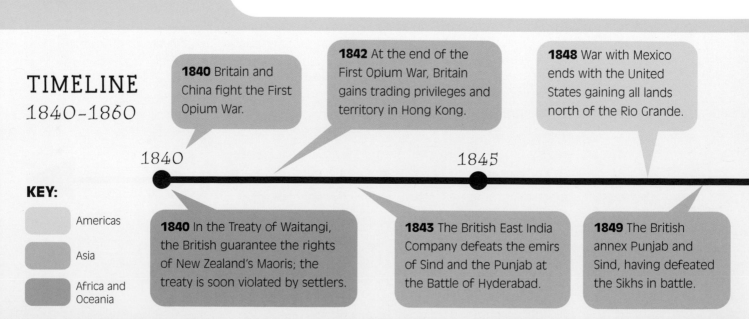

TIMELINE 1840–1860

1840 Britain and China fight the First Opium War.

1842 At the end of the First Opium War, Britain gains trading privileges and territory in Hong Kong.

1848 War with Mexico ends with the United States gaining all lands north of the Rio Grande.

1840 In the Treaty of Waitangi, the British guarantee the rights of New Zealand's Maoris; the treaty is soon violated by settlers.

1843 The British East India Company defeats the emirs of Sind and the Punjab at the Battle of Hyderabad.

1849 The British annex Punjab and Sind, having defeated the Sikhs in battle.

KEY:

Americas

Asia

Africa and Oceania

between the two white settler communities erupted later in the century in bitter Anglo-Boer wars.

France also embarked on colonization. It seized Algeria, a former Ottoman possession, in 1830, despire resistance. Eager for access to markets in Southeast Asia, France sent a force in 1858 to take Saigon. Four years later, the emperor of Annam was forced to cede control of eastern Cochin China to the foreigners. Over the next two decades, the French protectorate was extended to all of Vietnam and neighboring Cambodia.

↑ The Indian Mutiny broke out among Indian troops in the British army in 1857.

Yet there were failures, too. Emperor Napoleon III failed to take control of Mexico in 1863. Despite being embroiled in civil war, the United States forced the French to abandon the venture. The puppet emperor they had installed, Austria's Archduke Maximilian I, was deposed and executed. Warned off by the Monroe Doctrine, the European powers would make no further attempts to colonize the Americas.

Timeline (continued)

1857 After quelling the Indian Mutiny, the British transfer government of the subcontinent directly to the crown.

1859 Under their ambitious Emperor Napoleon III, the French capture Saigon in modern Vietnam, beginning their creation of the colony of Indochina.

1859 Spain overruns part of Morocco, beginning a presence in North Africa that leads to the establishment of Spanish Morocco in 1912.

1863 Napoleon III of France attempts to build an overseas empire in Mexico; the United States pressures French troops to withdraw in 1867.

c.1870 The discovery of gold and diamonds in southern Africa begins the "Scramble for Africa."

1852 Boer settlers in southern Africa found the republic of Transvaal.

1853 U.S. ships arrive at Edo, Japan, and force the Japanese to make a trade agreement with America.

1858 The British government takes control of the Indian subcontinent from the East India Company.

1855

1860

1850 California becomes the 31st state.

1857 The Indian Mutiny against British rule erupts.

1859 A joint Franco–Spanish force occupies Saigon, Vietnam; it marks the start of the French occupation of Southeast Asia.

The Scramble for Africa

The interior of Africa had largely escaped the attention of the outside world. In the 1870s, however, explorers penetrated to the heart of the "Dark Continent."

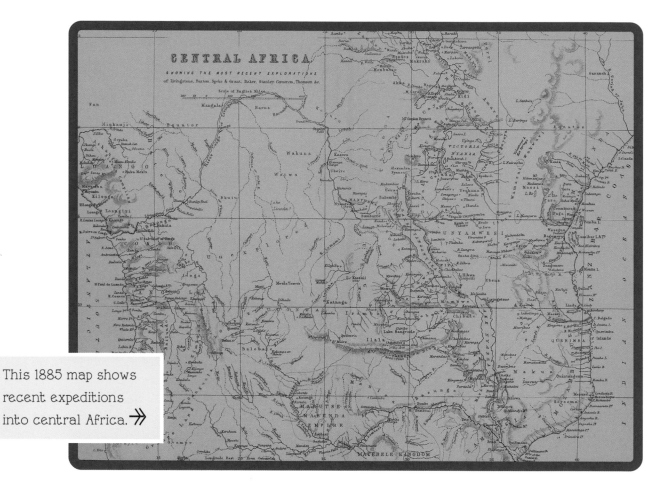

This 1885 map shows recent expeditions into central Africa. ➡

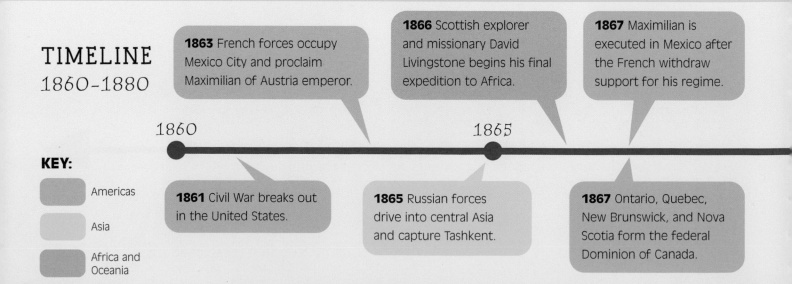

TIMELINE 1860–1880

KEY:

Americas

Asia

Africa and Oceania

1863 French forces occupy Mexico City and proclaim Maximilian of Austria emperor.

1866 Scottish explorer and missionary David Livingstone begins his final expedition to Africa.

1867 Maximilian is executed in Mexico after the French withdraw support for his regime.

1860

1865

1861 Civil War breaks out in the United States.

1865 Russian forces drive into central Asia and capture Tashkent.

1867 Ontario, Quebec, New Brunswick, and Nova Scotia form the federal Dominion of Canada.

In the seventeenth and eighteenth centuries Europe had known west Africa's coasts as a source of slaves and South Africa's Cape of Good Hope as a staging post for ships en route to India. In the nineteenth century, the situation changed radically: Despite is obvious benefits, the abolition of the slave trade brought chaos to the African kingdoms that relied on the trade.

↑ Livingstone visited Victoria Falls and named them for the British queen.

European nations—mainly Britain and France—offered individual states protection against their local enemies, gaining trade and political influence for themselves. Farther south, British expansion from the cape dislodged the region's Dutch-descended farmers. The Boers made their Great Trek inland into the territory of Transvaal.

Timeline of the Scramble for Africa

1805 Scottish explorer Mungo Park dies on the Niger River.

1807 Britain abolishes the slave trade.

1835 The Great Trek takes the Boers into the Transvaal.

1841 Scottish missionary David Livingstone begins a decade-long trek into central Africa.

1858 British explorers John Hanning Speke and Richard Burton reach Lake Tanganyika.

1862 Speke identifies Lake Victoria as the source of the White Nile.

1867 A major diamond find is made at Hopetown in Cape Colony.

← King Leopold ran the Belgian Congo as a private possession.

1873 The British reform the Indian Raj to allow local people more control.

1876 New Zealand is united as a dominion of the British empire.

1880 The First Boer War begins when Transvaal's Boers declare their independence from Britain.

1875

1880

1871 Reporter Henry Morton Stanley tracks down the explorer David Livingstone, who has been missing in east Africa for several years.

1875 Britain becomes the majority owner of the Suez Canal.

1877 Britain annexes Transvaal in South Africa.

Timeline (continued)

1868 French colonists establish a protectorate in Ivory Coast.

1876 Leopold II of Belgium establishes the International African Association.

1881 The French occupy Tunisia.

1882 British forces occupy Egypt.

1884 The Berlin Conference addresses conflicting European claims to African territory.

1885 Germany annexes East Africa (now Tanzania).

→ Between 1880 and World War I, Africa was transformed into a patchwork of European colonies.

A series of explorers were meanwhile helping open up Africa to exploitation, even though that was rarely their intention. Mungo Park traveled up the Niger River; missionary David Livingstone reached the heart of the continent; and Richard Burton and John Hanning Speke visited the Great Lakes region, looking for the source of the Nile.

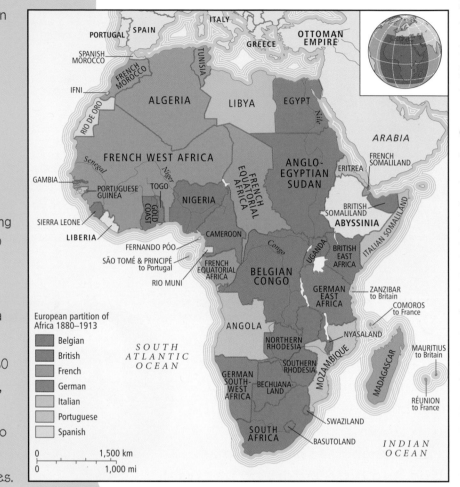

European partition of Africa 1880–1913

- Belgian
- British
- French
- German
- Italian
- Portuguese
- Spanish

0   1,500 km
0   1,000 mi

Oppression

The mapping of a region often preceded a colonial claim. King Leopold II of Belgium took a leading role; he built up a private kingdom in the Congo Basin that became infamous for its brutality toward Africans.

By the 1880s, unclaimed lands

TIMELINE 1880–1900

1882 British forces occupy Egypt at the request of its Ottoman governor.

1885 The Indian National Congress is formed to campaign for independence from Britain.

1889 The Italians make a treaty with Ethiopia, which they interpret as allowing them to set up a colonial protectorate.

1880

1885

1881 At the end of the First Boer War, Britain makes concessions to the Boers of Transvaal.

1885 Leopold II of Belgium becomes the personal ruler of Congo Free State; millions of Africans die in the brutal colonization that follows.

1889 France establishes a protectorate in Ivory Coast.

KEY:

- Americas
- Asia
- Africa and Oceania

in Africa were pawns in a complex struggle for national prestige among the major European powers. Britain and France were the first main players; British dreams of a north–south empire stretching "from the Cape to Cairo" clashed with French ambitions for a band of colonies reaching from the Atlantic to the Indian Ocean. From 1878 on, Germany made its voice heard, establishing protectorates in Togo and Cameroon as well as in east and southwest Africa. Italy laid claim to Somaliland and Eritrea, but its plans to take over Ethiopia also were crushed when its army went down to defeat at Adowa in 1896.

By that time, much of the continent had been parceled out among European governments with little knowledge or understanding of African populations. As the name suggests, the Scramble for Africa was largely unplanned and opportunistic. Its legacy was a continent whose traditional societies were disrupted in pursuit of European interests.

PUNCH, OR THE LONDON CHARIVARI. [December 10, 189

266

THE RHODES COLOSSUS
STRIDING FROM CAPE TOWN TO CAIRO.

Timeline (continued)

1885 Leopold II of Belgium sets up the Congo Free State.

1885 Followers of the Mahdi take Khartoum, Sudan. The killing of General Gordon causes outrage in Britain.

1890 Zanzibar becomes a British protectorate.

1895 The territory of the British South Africa Company is named Rhodesia in honor of Cecil Rhodes.

1896 An Italian attempt to seize Ethiopia is defeated at the Battle of Adowa.

1899 The Second Boer War breaks out between British and Boer settlers in southern Africa.

↑ British empire-builder Cecil Rhodes bestrides Africa; Rhodes planned a railroad to stretch across the continent.

1890 Cecil Rhodes becomes prime minister of South Africa's Cape Colony.

1896 The British establish protectorates in Sierra Leone and east Africa.

1897 German forces establish a trading post in China.

1898 The United States annexes Hawaii.

1895

1900

1893 New Zealand becomes the first country to give women the right to vote in national elections.

1896 After being defeated in the Battle of Adowa, Italy is forced to recognize the independence of Ethiopia.

1898 Britain obtains a lease from China for Kowloon, the mainland territory neighboring Hong Kong.

Glossary

alliance An agreement between two groups or countries to cooperate for the purposes of defense or economic growth.

annex To take possession of an area of land previously occupied or claimed by another country.

caste system The traditional Indian social system which separates the population into classes defined by family background and occupation.

cede The act of granting a territory or state to another country.

circumnavigation Traveling all the way around the world by boat. The term is also used to describe a journey around an island or continent.

colony A country or region under the direct control of another country.

conquistador A Spanish soldier involved in the exploration and conquest of the Americas.

constitution A set of rules by which a government operates.

debtor A person who owes a significant amount of money to another person or institution; often used to describe someone who is unable or unwilling to pay the money back.

independence A separation of a colony from the country which formerly controlled it.

indigenous A term used to describe a people or species that was already living in a region before settlers arrived.

mutiny A rebellion by members of the military against their commanding officers.

navigator A person who guides a ship or aircraft to its intended destination using charts, logs, and navigational instruments.

opium A highly addictive drug extracted from the seed pods of opium poppies, which grow in Central Asia.

outback The largely inhospitable inland regions of the Australian continent.

penal A type of colony where the settlers are criminals forcibly deported from their home country.

protectorate A form of colonization in which a country surrenders some of its autonomy to a more powerful country in exchange for military support.

spices Dried seeds, leaves, or roots that can be added to food as a flavoring or preservative. Spices were extremely valuable during the age of exploration.

Further Reading

Books

Berne, Emma Carlson. *Christopher Columbus: The Voyage That Changed the World*. New York: Sterling, 2008.

Burkholder, Mark A., and Lyman L. Johnson. *Colonial Latin America*. New York: Oxford University Press, 2007.

Eakin, Marshall C. *The History of Latin America: Collision of Cultures*. New York: Palgrave Macmillan, 2007.

Gilbert, Erik, and Jonathan T. Reynolds. *Africa in World History*. Upper Saddle River, NJ: Prentice Hall, 2007.

Horwitz, Tony. *A Voyage Long and Strange: Rediscovering the New World*. New York: Henry Holt and Co., 2008.

Iliffe, John. *Africans: The History of a Continent*. New York: Cambridge University Press, 2007.

Johnson, Michael. *Encyclopedia of Native Tribes of North America*. London: Firefly Books, 2007.

Keen, Benjamin, and Keith Haynes. *A History of Latin America*. Boston: Wadsworth Publishing, 2008.

Lindsay, Lisa A. *Captives as Commodities: The Transatlantic Slave Trade*. Upper Saddle River, NJ: Prentice Hall, 2007.

Reynolds, Henry. *The Other Side of the Frontier: Aboriginal Resistance to the European Invasion of Australia*. Sydney: University of New South Wales Press, 2007.

Taylor, Alan. *American Colonies: The Settling of North America*. New York: Penguin Books, 2002.

Wood, Gordon S. *The American Revolution: A History*. New York: Modern Library, 2003.

Wood, Michael. *Conquistadors*. Berkeley: University of California Press, 2002.

Zeitz, Amy, and Johannes Postma. *The Atlantic Slave Trade*. Gainesville: University Press of Florida, 2005.

Web Sites

www.kidinfo.com/American_History/ Colonization_Colonial_Life.html
Links to sites providing information about life in the American colonies

www.eyewitnesstohistory.com/ 18frm.htm
Firsthand accounts of many events from colonial America and the Revolutionary War

www.cybrary.org/colonial.htm
Offers information about individual American colonies

Index